Mary Cohen & Robert Spearing

Quartetstart

Level 2

Original repertoire for established beginner string quartets

© 1999 by Faber Music Ltd
First published in 1999 by Faber Music Ltd
3 Queen Square London WC1N 3AU
Cover design by S & M Tucker
Music processed by Mary Cohen and Jackie Leigh
Printed in England by Caligraving Ltd

ISBN 0-571-51943-1

To buy Faber Music publications or to find out about the full range of titles available
please contact your local retailer or Faber Music sales enquiries:

Faber Music Ltd, Burnt Mill, Elizabeth Way, Harlow CM20 2HX
Tel: +44 (0)1279 82 89 82   Fax: +44 (0)1279 82 89 83
sales@fabermusic.com   www.fabermusic.com

Contents

To the teacher

Quartetstart Level 2 is designed for young players whose individual standard is about grade (AB) 2–3 and who have some string quartet experience. There is a wide variety of styles and textures and each piece has a clearly defined character, telling a story or painting a picture in sound. With the exception of occasional one-octave harmonics, the material throughout the book is written in first finger pattern (for example, violin: 0 1 23 4) or second finger pattern (0 12 3 4), enabling the group to concentrate on the development of musical and ensemble skills. The rehearsal tips in the score are intended to be read out and discussed. Each individual part contains little technique tips throughout to help deal with problems which might otherwise disrupt the musical flow. As in *Quartetstart Level 1*, multiple bars rest are written out with 'One 234, Two 234', etc. being added to aid counting and to encourage players to make confident entries.

Mary Cohen

Recommended background material

Mixed duet experience:
Superduets 1 for violin and cello (beginner)
Superduets 2 for violin and cello (established beginner – grade 1)

Quartet experience:
Quartetstart Level 1 (grade 1–2)
Christmas Quartetstart (grade 1–2+)

All of the above titles are in Mary Cohen's *Superseries*
and are available from Faber Music.

Festive Fanfare

Keep the tempo lively throughout. This is in 'call and response' style, so it's a conversation between all four players. As you get to know the music, work out who you are 'calling out' with or 'responding' to, then you can glance at each other as you make your entries. Bar 22 is a general pause – a whole bar rest for everyone – so count carefully together, looking at each other if possible.

Mary Cohen

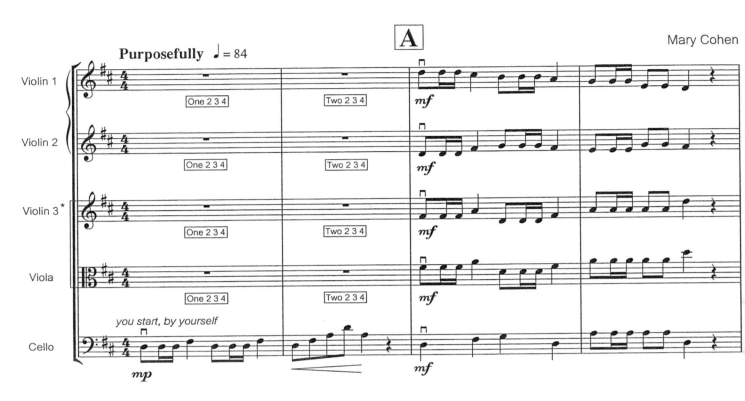

* Violin 3: alternative to Viola

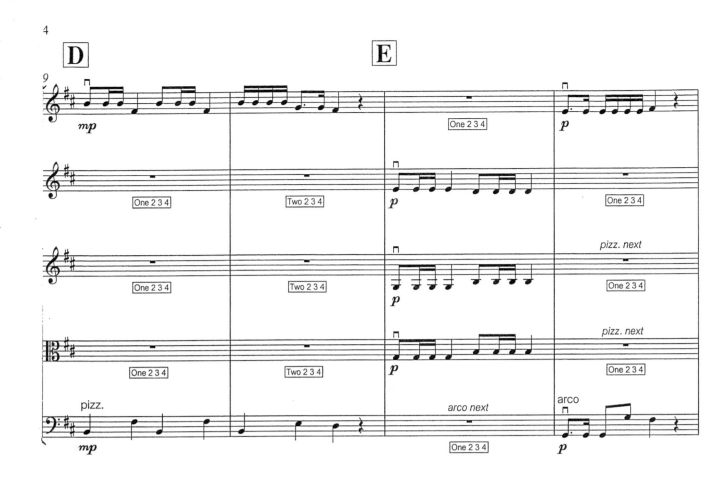

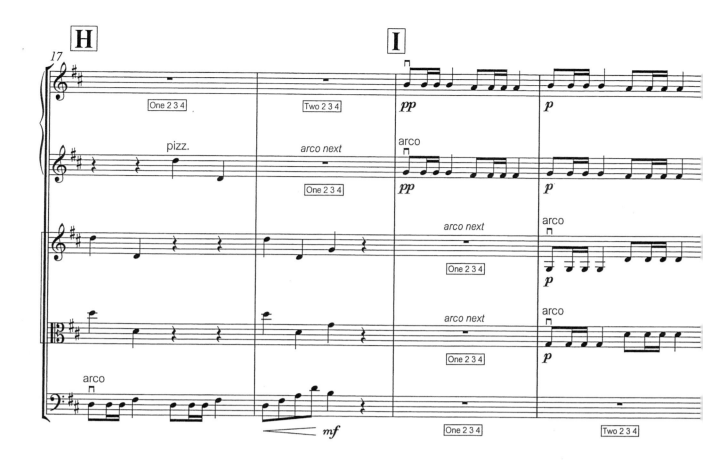

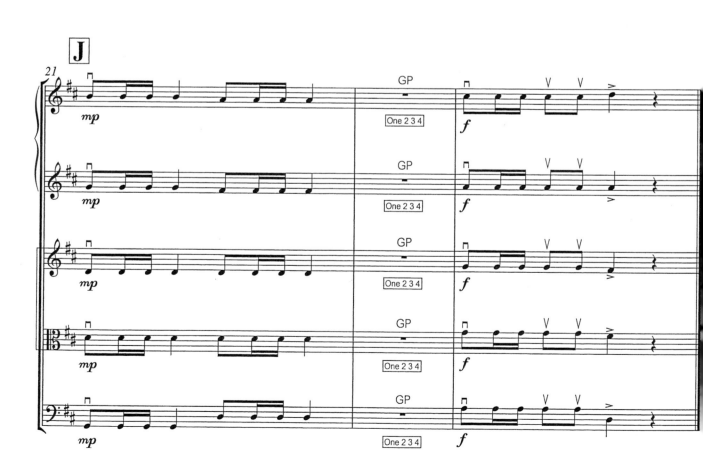

Video diary

1. The old tyre and some rope make an excellent swing

There are several little 'duets' going on in this piece. Listen to two players at a time in various combinations, e.g. just the 2nd violin and cello or 1st violin and 3rd violin/viola in bars 1-8. What other interesting combinations are there? Keep the feeling of 'swinging' by staying absolutely rhythmic and in tempo throughout, especially in bars with rests or long notes.

Mary Cohen

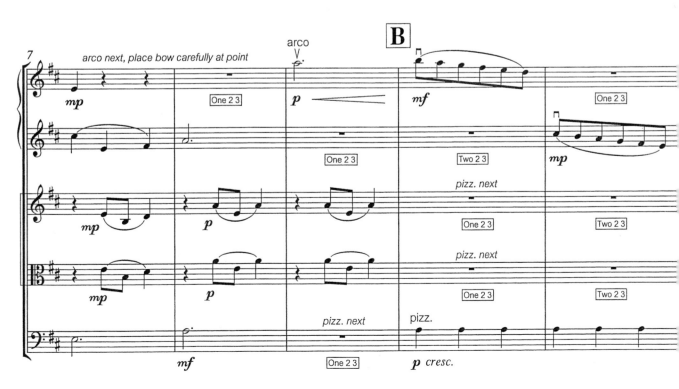

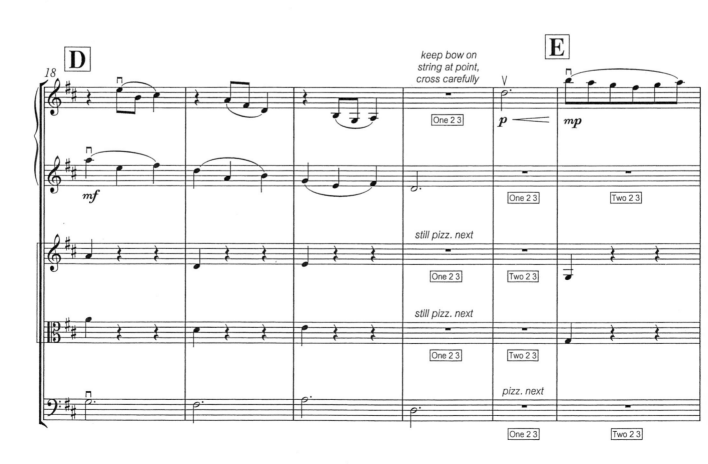

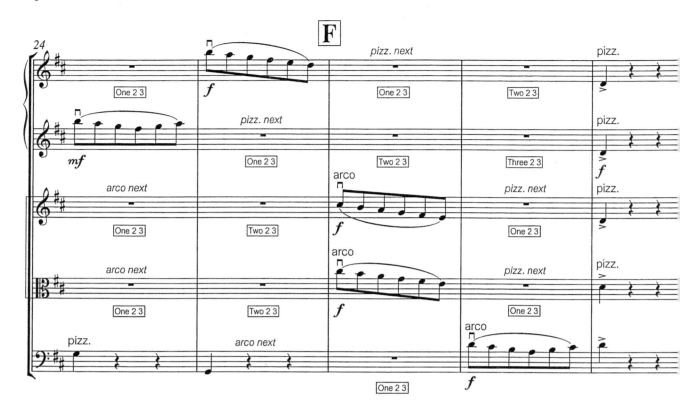

2. Before breakfast, we jog 'marathons' around the garden

A virtuoso 'marathon' for the cellist – you'll never find it hard to play bottom D ever again
if you master this piece. Everyone needs to listen to everyone else all the time to keep it
absolutely together. Let the cellist have a rest occasionally and rehearse the other three parts.

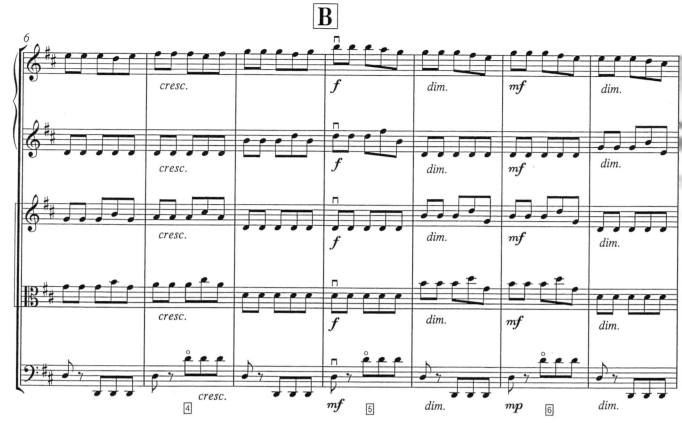

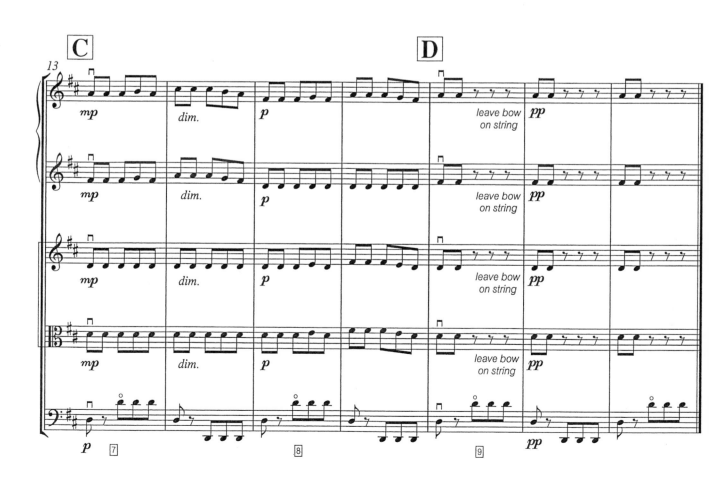

3. Our cousins show us how to skim stones across water so they bounce and bounce

A busy soundscape with stones skimming and bouncing or dropping into the water. Once again there are several 'duet' partnerships running through the piece. Listen to four bars at a time with different combinations of two players. Follow all the bowing instructions carefully.

Mary Cohen

Victorian Seaside Holiday

'Place' carefully every note which follows a staccato – e.g. bar 2 in 1st and 2nd violins. Take particular care placing the last notes of bars 15 and 16. There is an interesting 'special effect' in the dynamics at D, E, J, N and O – a subito (sudden) *piano* or *pianissimo* after a *crescendo*. This needs very good bow control and a lot of practice!

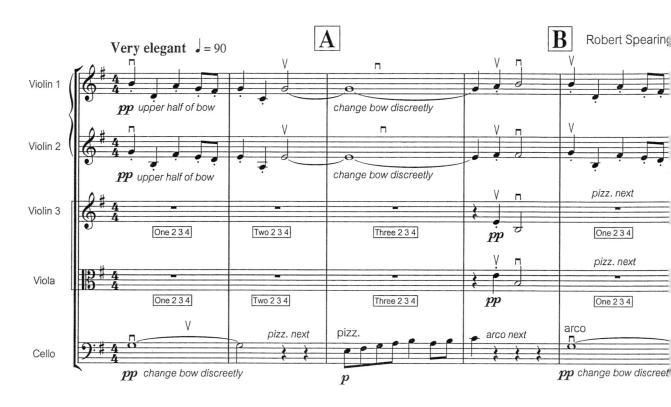

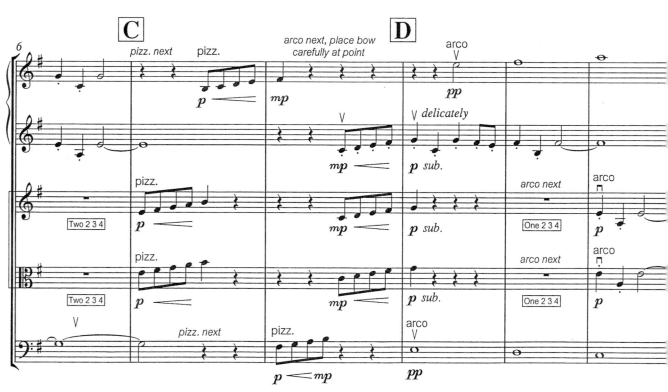

Sing it 'n' swing it

Mary Cohen

Cello

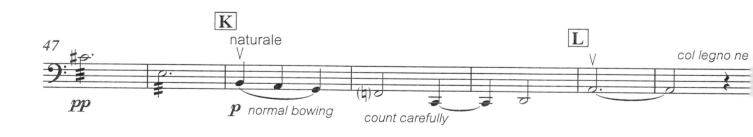

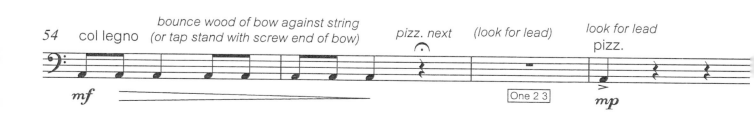

Waltz of the Skeletons

Relaxed tempo ♩ = 126

Robert Spearing

con sord. *(muted throughout)*

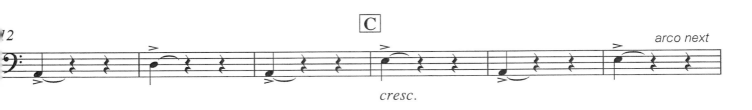

Cello

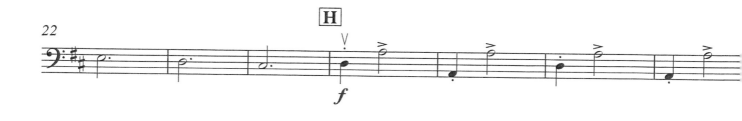

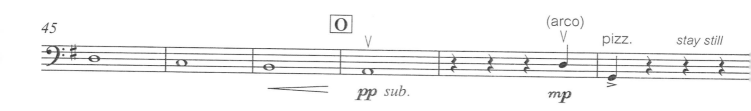

Cello

Victorian Seaside Holiday

Robert Spearing

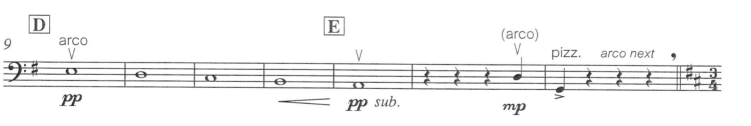

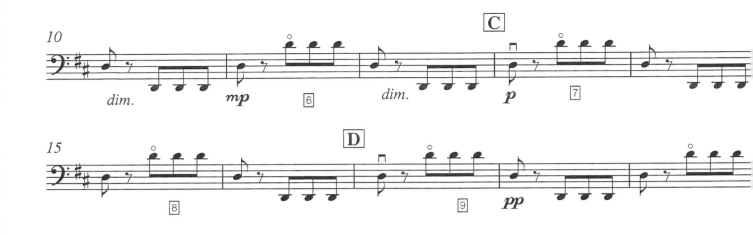

3. Our cousins show us how to skim stones across water so they bounce and bounce

With steady movement ♩ = 80

Mary Cohe

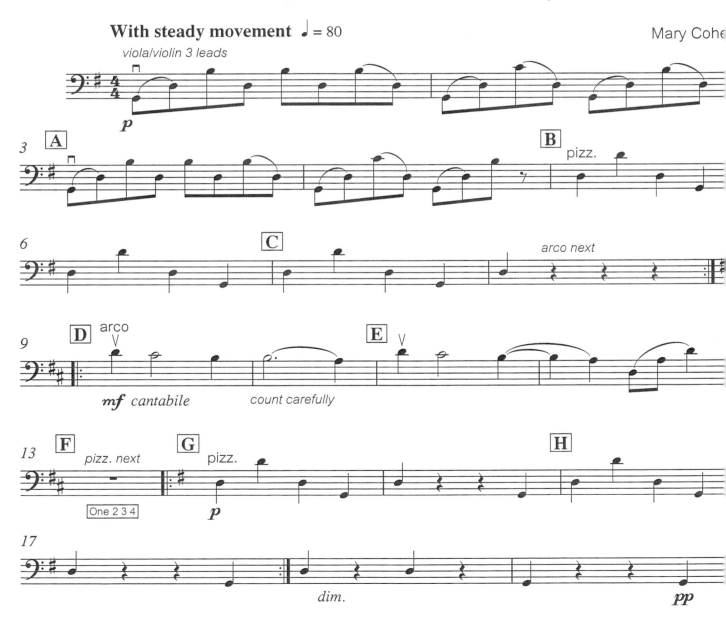

Video diary

1. The old tyre and some rope make an excellent swing

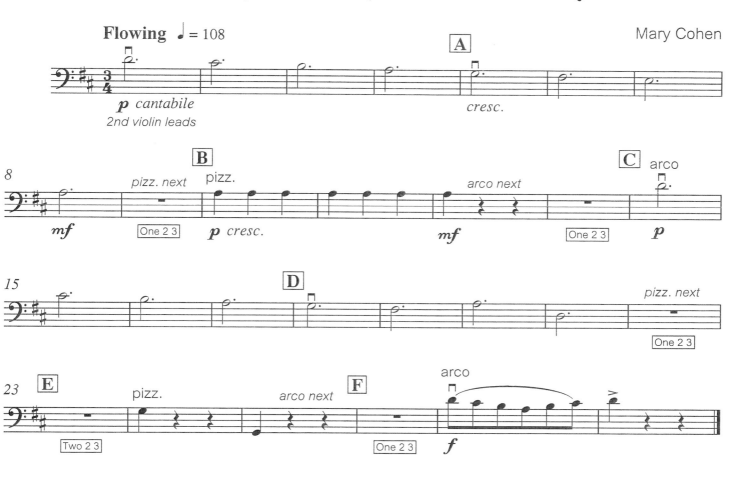

2. Before breakfast, we jog 'marathons' around the garden

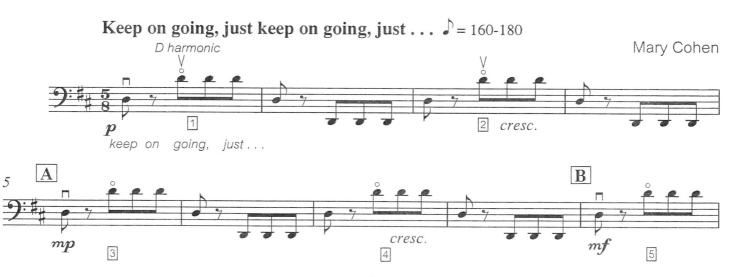

Cello

Festive Fanfare

Mary Cohen

Sing it 'n' swing it

Mary Cohen

Viola

Waltz of the Skeletons

Relaxed tempo ♩ = 126

Robert Spearing

Viola

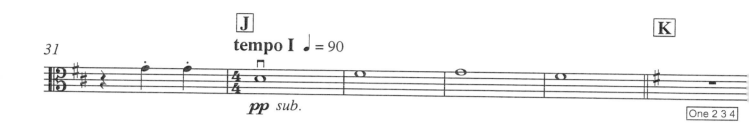

Victorian Seaside Holiday

Robert Spearing

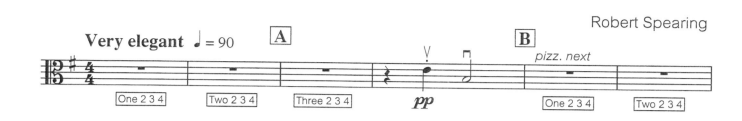

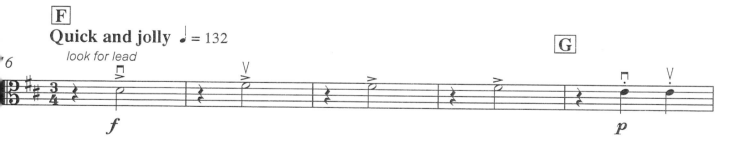

cresc.

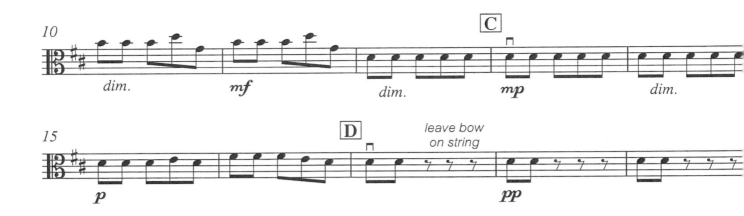

3. Our cousins show us how to skim stones across water so they bounce and bounce

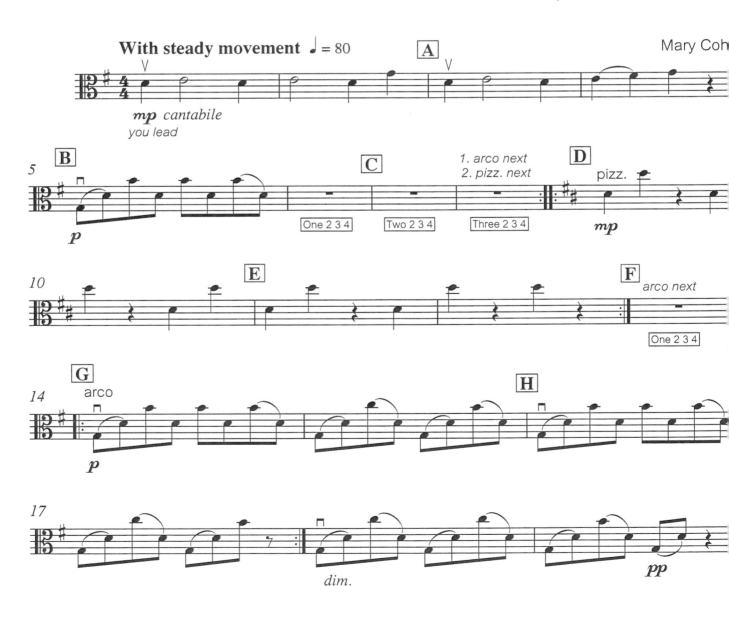

Mary Coh

Video diary

1. The old tyre and some rope make an excellent swing

Mary Cohen

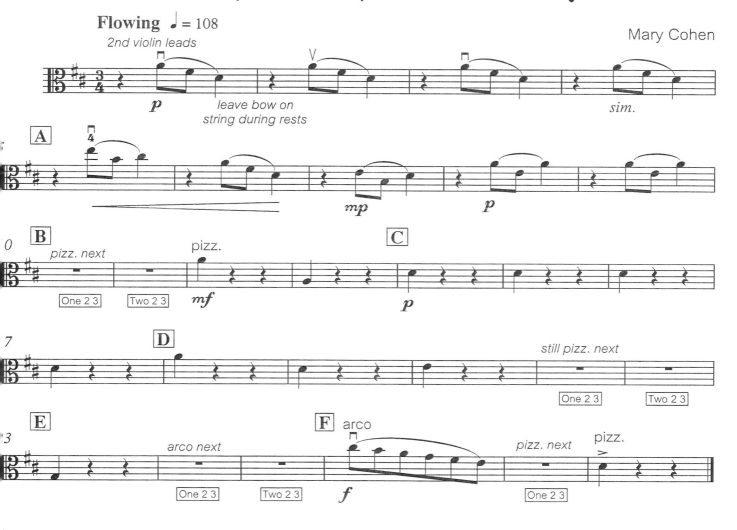

2. Before breakfast, we jog 'marathons' around the garden

Mary Cohen

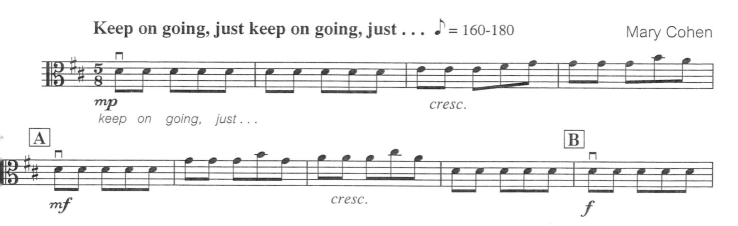

Festive Fanfare

Viola

Mary Coh

Sing it 'n' swing it

Mary Cohen

Violin 3

Waltz of the Skeletons

Robert Spearing

Violin 3

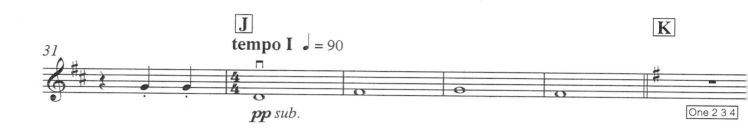

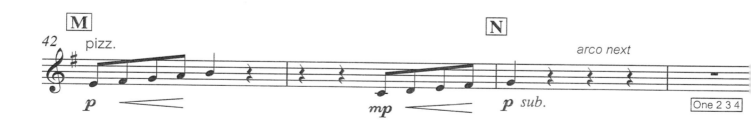

Victorian Seaside Holiday

Robert Spearing

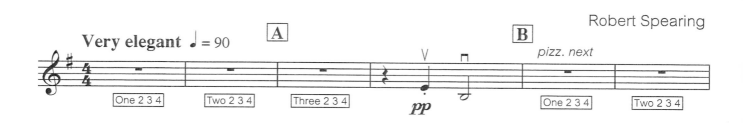

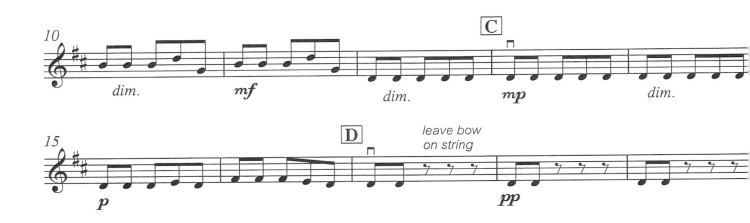

3. Our cousins show us how to skim stones across water so they bounce and bounce

Video diary

1. The old tyre and some rope make an excellent swing

Mary Cohen

2. Before breakfast, we jog 'marathons' around the garden

Mary Cohen

Festive Fanfare

Violin 3
(alternative to Viola)

Mary Coh

Sing it 'n' swing it

With a swing ♩ = 120   Mary Cohen

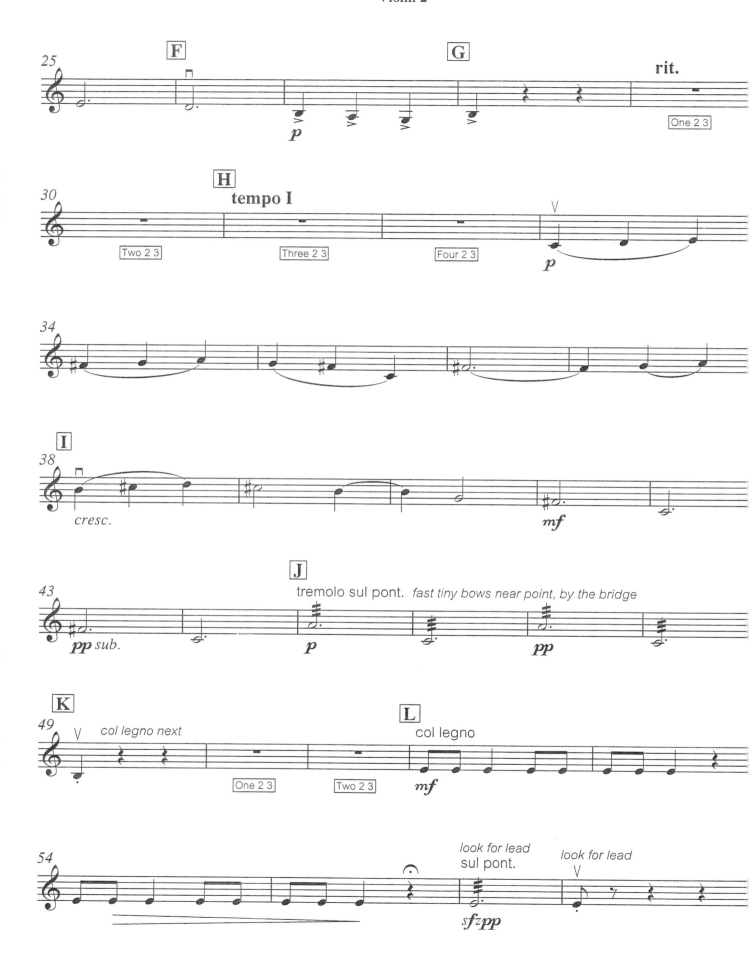

Waltz of the Skeletons

Robert Spearing

Violin 2

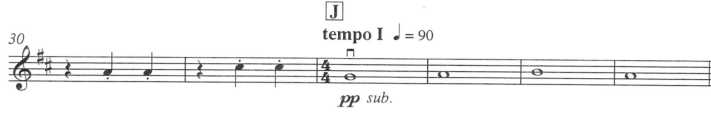

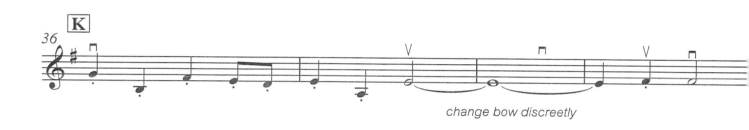

Victorian Seaside Holiday

Robert Spearing

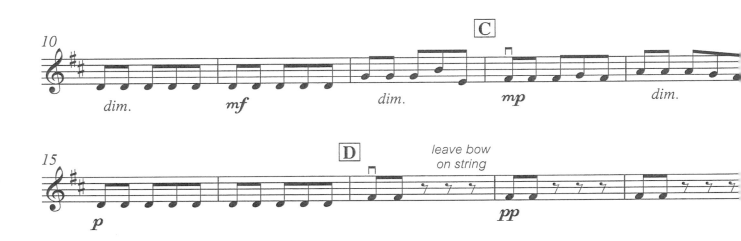

3. Our cousins show us how to skim stones across water so they bounce and bounce

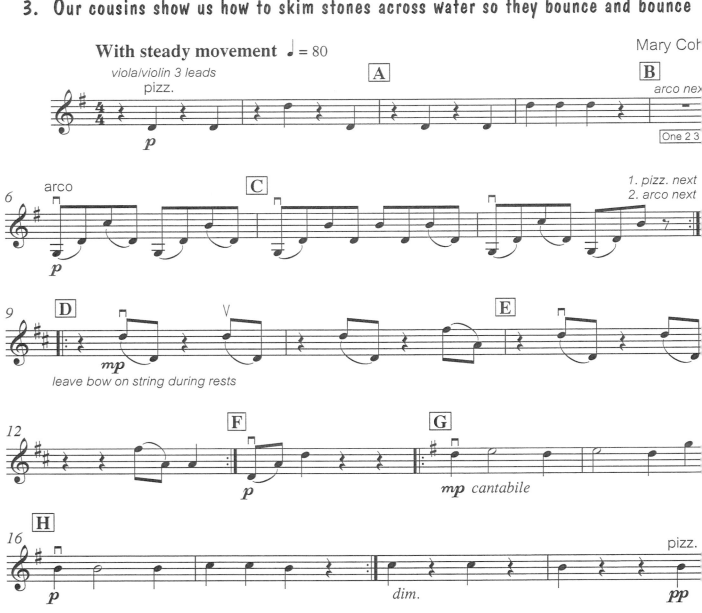

Video diary

1. The old tyre and some rope make an excellent swing

Mary Cohen

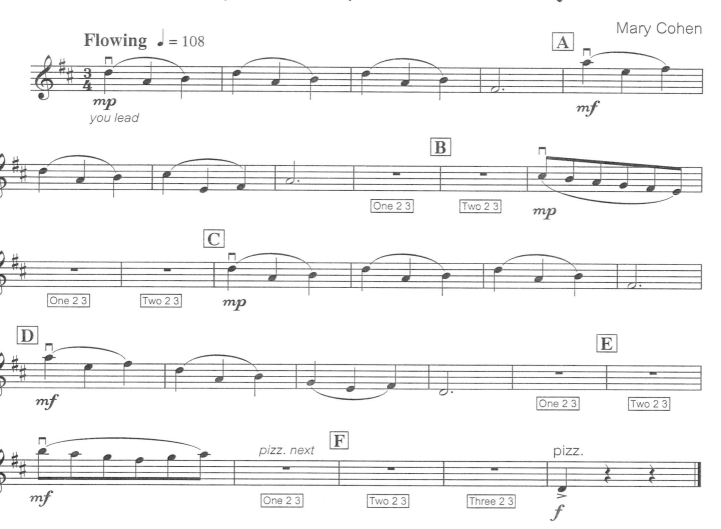

2. Before breakfast, we jog 'marathons' around the garden

Mary Cohen

Violin 2

Festive Fanfare

Mary Coh[...]

Sing it 'n' swing it

Mary Cohen

Violin 1

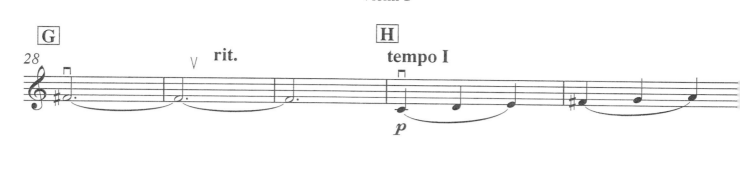

Waltz of the Skeletons

Robert Spearing

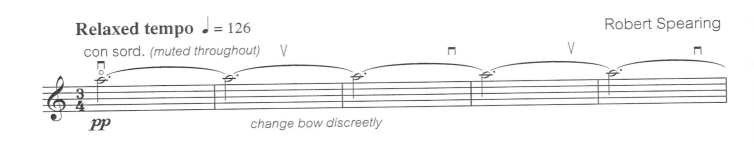

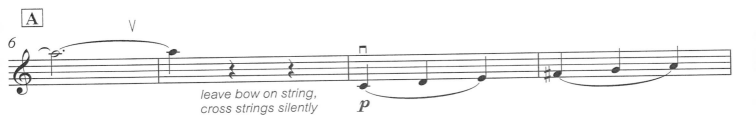

Violin 1

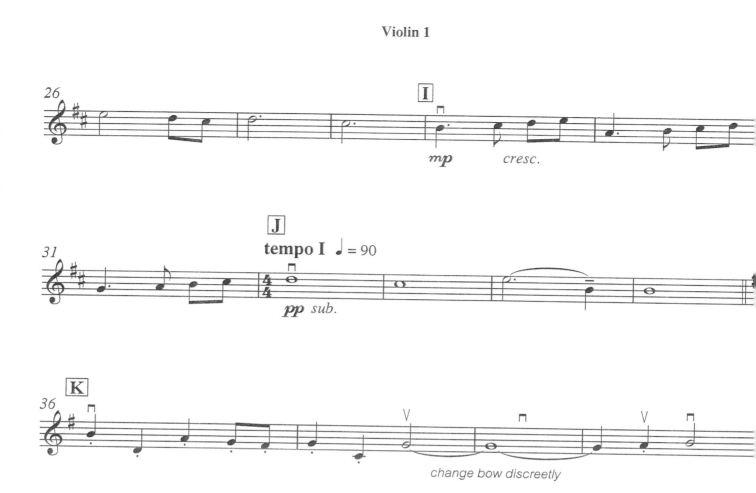

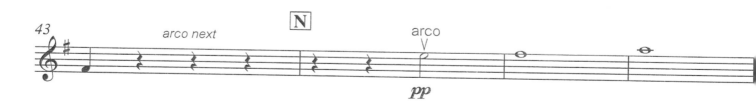

Victorian Seaside Holiday

Robert Spearing

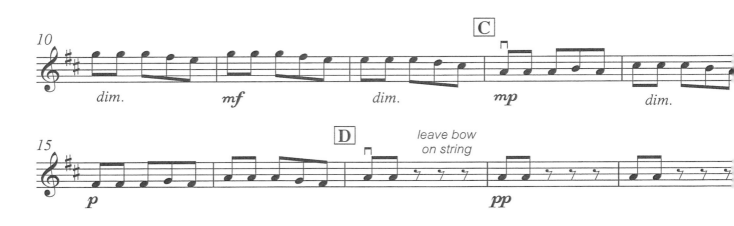

3. Our cousins show us how to skim stones across water so they bounce and bounce

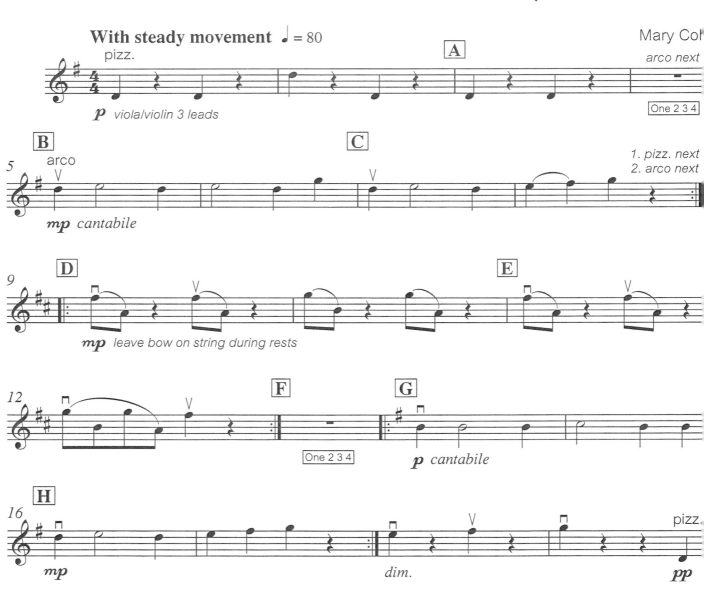

Video diary

1. The old tyre and some rope make an excellent swing

Mary Cohen

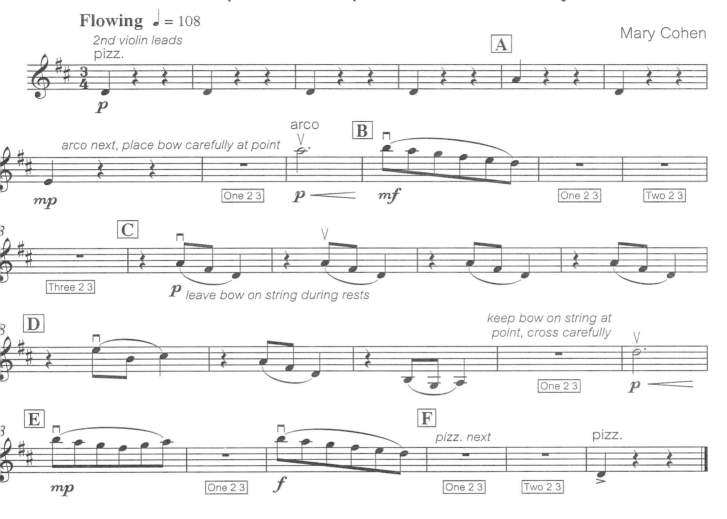

2. Before breakfast, we jog 'marathons' around the garden

Mary Cohen

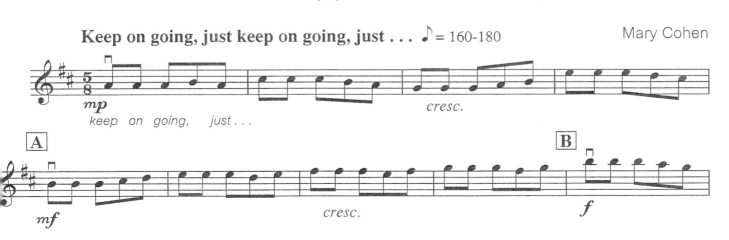

Violin 1

Festive Fanfare

Mary Coh

E

F **Quick and jolly** ♩ = 132

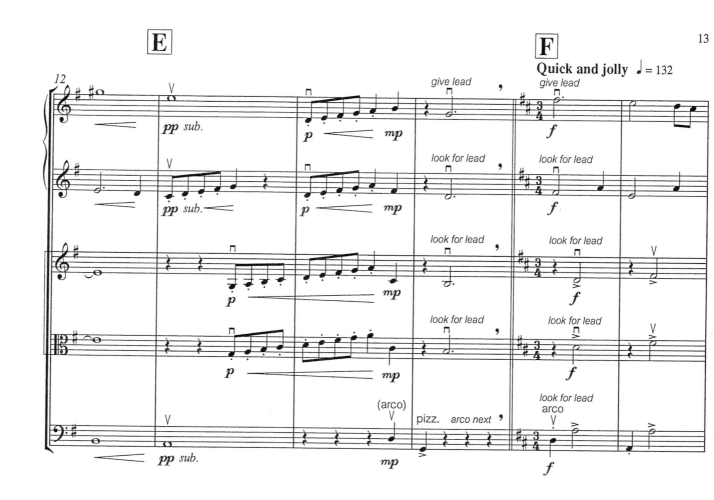

G

14

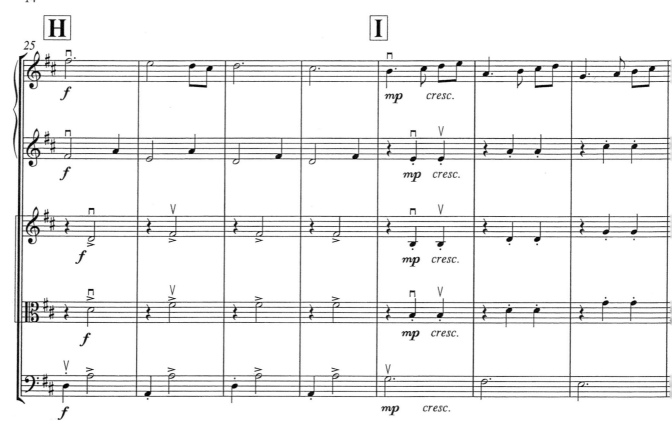

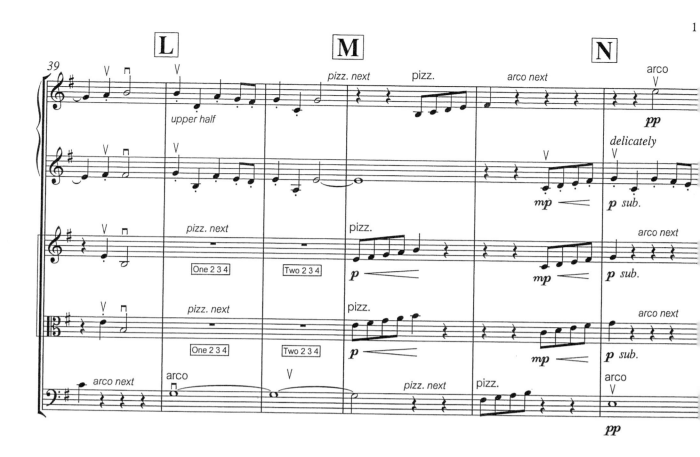

Waltz of the Skeletons

Lots of special effects here, so make sure the tune can always be heard against the background of eerie held notes, rattling skeletons, spooky ringing pizzicatos and icy cold tremolos. An alternative to the col legno is tapping the screw end of the bow on the stand.

Robert Spearing

* in parts: bounce wood of bow against string

C

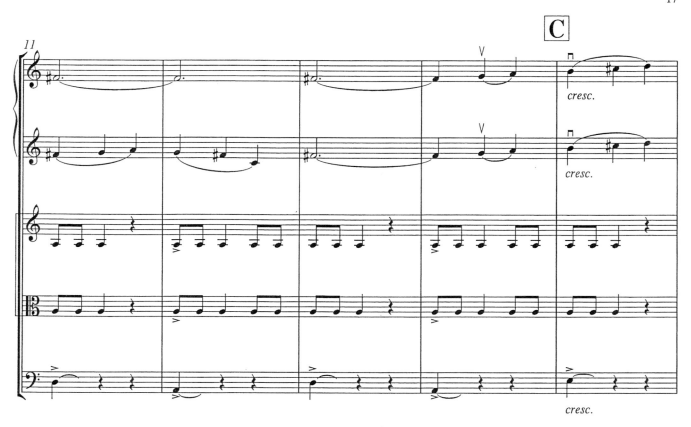

D

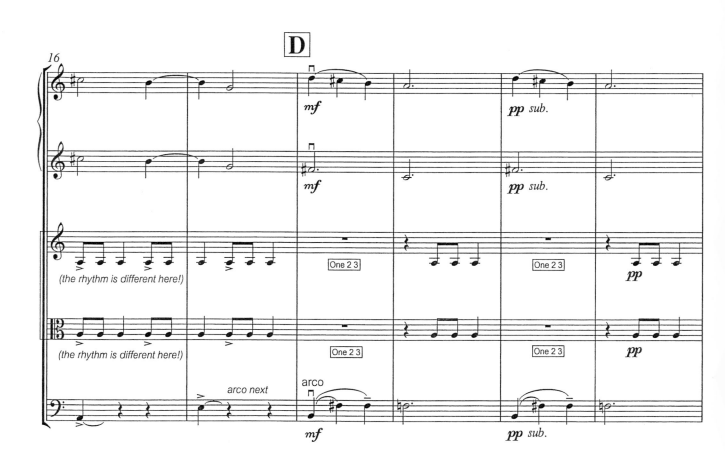

18

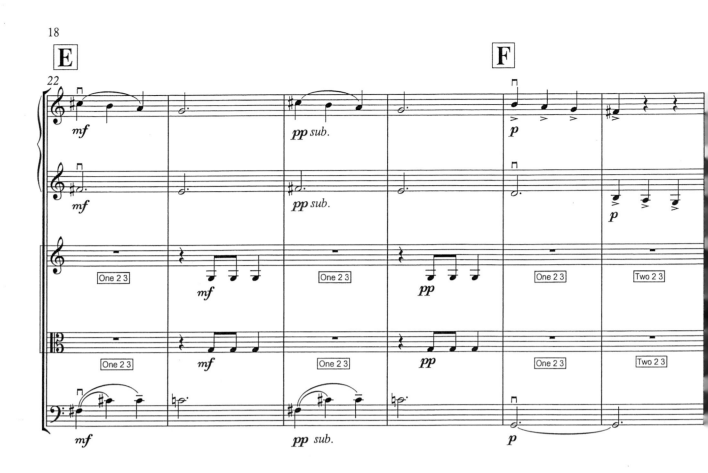

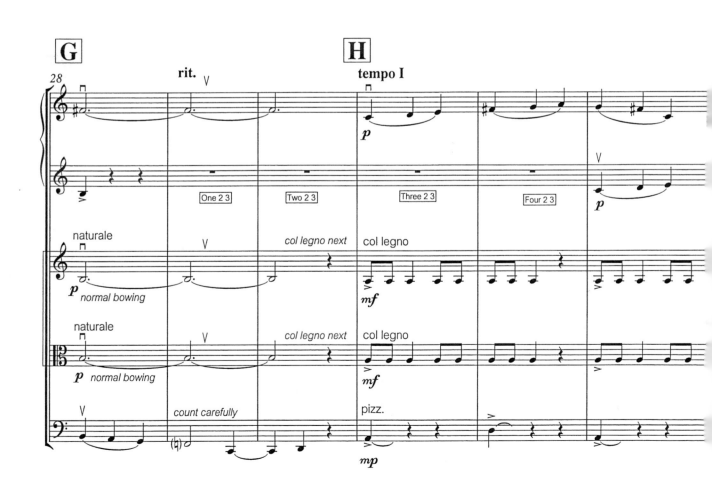

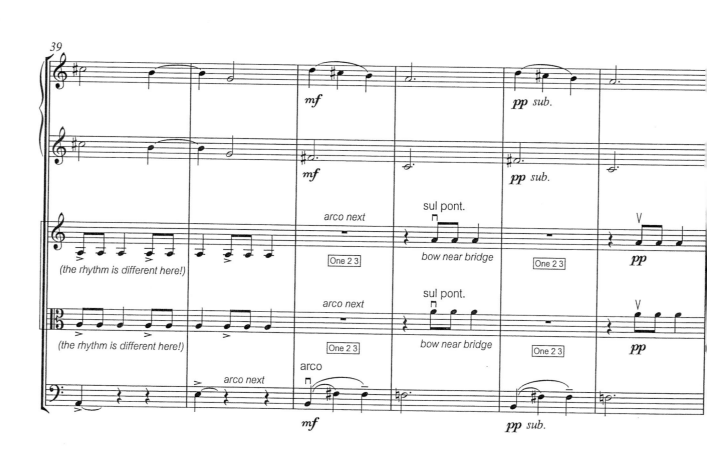

20

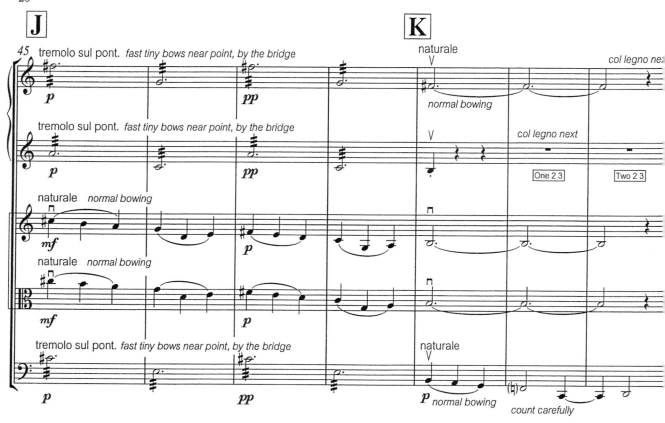

Sing it 'n' swing it

With the exception of the very last bar, the rhythm of everything else fits either the words 'Doo be doo be doo' or 'Rum bah ba' so 'think' these phrases all the way through instead of counting '1,2,3,4'. The words written as examples under some of the bars are to help with rehearsing, but not meant to be sung during the final performance. You'll soon get the 'Charleston' and 'Rumba' swing – especially if you start by reading through small sections without instruments, just singing or saying the appropriate words.

Mary Cohen

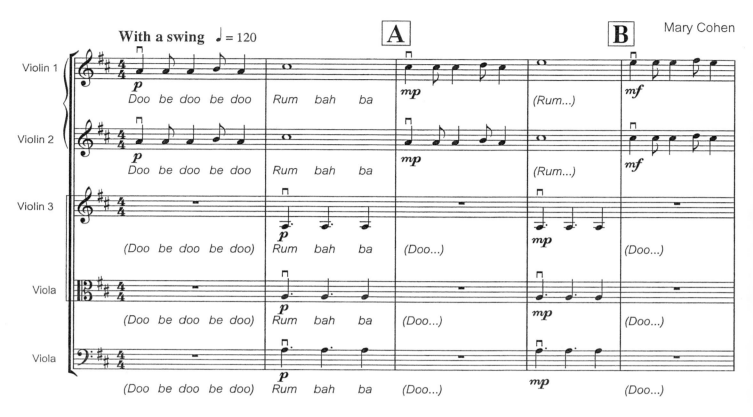

23